The Seven Laws of Achievement

How to Achieve Success in Life

David L. Cain

© Three One 6 LLC
35 Woodrun Court
Easton, Pa, 18042
www.threeone6.com

Edited by Patricia L Magnus, Magnus Books
Sarasota, FL, USA

First Edition published March 2013.
Printed in the United States of America

10 9 8 7 6 5 4 3 2 1

ISBN: 978-0-9889174-0-8

© 2013 Three One 6 LLC

Preface

The year was 1998 and the city was Detroit. Boldly pursuing the vision that was shared with me by a close friend, I started a nonprofit organization called the Minority Enhancement Network (known as MEN). MEN's objective was to help male teens whose fathers did not live with them or were not present in their lives. The young men who participated in the program were between the ages 8 and 18, lived in homes headed by a single parent (always a female), and were socioeconomically disadvantaged.

We worked with our members via workshops and mentoring arrangements and we called the latter The Making of an Eagle workshop. We taught everything from basic life survival skills to the importance of education during each of the workshop's two day meetings.

One of these sessions is indelibly etched in my mind to this day. The session began like any other, but one of the participants was a bit extraordinary. He had come from juvenile detention. According to his file, he had been placed there because he had shot someone. We were told that our workshop was a last ditch attempt to rehabilitate him in any fashion – all else had failed.

In the middle of the workshop, this particular young man

got up and over to the window and just started staring up at the sky. I walked over and asked him if he was okay. With tears in his eyes, he nodded. He could barely get the words out, but he told me that it was his younger brother who needed to be part of our workshop.

I asked why and he told me that his little brother was drug dealing drugs on the street. The young man was afraid that his younger sibling would end up in a worse situation than he was in. My answer was to advise him that if he wanted to help his brother, he needed to lead by example. He needed to himself be the change that he wanted his brother to be. I never met his brother, and my program continued for many years, successfully helping hundreds of disadvantaged male youths through to the year 2000.

Years later in 2002, I had an extraordinary experience in quite an ordinary place. I pulled into a Kmart parking lot, again in Detroit. It was dark and I walked past a large man. I tried to walk quickly, but the man turned to me and asked if I knew him.

In certain sections of Detroit at the time, such an inquiry was often an opening for trouble. I said, "No, I'm sorry, I don't know you."

He asked again, "Are you sure you don't know me." I answered that I did not.

After I said I didn't know him, he challenged me further; his name did not ring a bell to me. I was getting nervous here, until the pleasantly shocking revelation that Tre was that very kid who had stood at the window crying years before.

Then he shocked me by telling me that he was the kid that stood at the window crying during one of our workshops. Amazed, I asked what he was doing with his life. He said he was a college student and worked at Kmart part time. I was impressed. He was in school, and he had a job. Then came the revelation, straight from the lips of Tre, "I wouldn't be here doing this if I hadn't gone to that workshop. I learned a lot there." We talked for a while, and I didn't even go into Kmart. I went home, tears of joy filling my heart.

This young man was taught, in that little workshop those many years ago, the same skills that I am now setting down in print for you. Tre is a living example of what following the seven laws of achievement can achieve. If he can do it, so can you.

Why the Seven Laws of Achievement?

"You can't teach what you don't know and can't lead where you won't go." These are the words my preacher spoke in the introduction to his sermon on a recent Sunday morning. Later, he would explain that the adage should always be referenced when considering feedback or advice provided by others. His point was that advice is most valuable when it comes from someone who has deep knowledge of a subject or firsthand experience. For example, I have very little knowledge or experience as a concert pianist and would question the sanity of anyone who accepted my guidance on the topic.

Over the years, I have often hailed the preacher's advice, using the sound maxim as a launching pad, just as he recommended. More importantly, I also use it to determine whether or not I am qualified to give guidance to others. Over the years, I have seen countless numbers of bad decisions made because of selection failure. This is not to say that the right decision can only come from someone steep in knowledge or firsthand experience. My mother barely had a high school education, yet she imparted advice and wisdom that I listened to as if it had come from King Solomon himself.

Thus, *The Seven Laws of Achievement* is the result of acquired knowledge and firsthand experiences. It represents a formula for success that has seen me through three decades of personal, professional, corporate, and community achievement.

The first of these decades was in the 1970s, and I was in my teens. My favorite television show was *Good Times*[i], a fictional tale of an African-American family that lived in one of the projects in Chicago. Their struggles may have been fictional, but they were very real to me. Looking back now, I can honestly say that I lived the old joke that "we were so poor that the only thing I could pay (for) was attention." I may laugh about it now, but it wasn't funny back then.

It wasn't funny because we weren't happy, or at least that's how it seemed at the time. The Constitution guarantees the right of every American the pursuit of happiness, but as Benjamin Franklin quipped "it's up to you to catch it." I don't know anything about the neighborhood that Mr. Franklin lived in, but in the tough neighborhood of my youth the pursuit of happiness was littered with one obstacle after another.

Role models were few and far between. Neither my school system nor my community offered the type of services my family needed to help us catch that right. My neighborhood had its share of drugs and crime, and according to the statistics of the day, any male youth between the ages of 16 and 24 who grew up there was likely to end up with at least a lengthy jail record, and at worst, early death. The odds were heavily stacked against me. The only jobs available were in the hard labor category, and these paid a pittance. For a family that included six children, a recipe for failure, setback, and disappointment was well in place.

Though I had two older brothers and one older sister, I was the first in my immediate family to graduate from high school – a fact that haunts me to this very day. My elder siblings dropped out of high school and never had a fighting chance of coming close to sampling the American dream. Every day I wish for a time machine so that I can go back in time and share the Seven Laws of Achievement with my family. If they knew what I know now, I'm sure their lives would have turned out quite differently.

Today, I am a senior leader for a large multinational pharmaceutical company and am responsible for supporting more than 15 drug manufacturing sites in emerging market countries. These countries include Africa, Algiers, Argentina, Brazil, China, Egypt, India, Indonesia, Japan Mexico, Russia, Senegal, Turkey, and Tunisia. Following my passion for helping others achieve their goals, I have consulted with and advised many business and non-profit leaders at the domestic and international level helping them achieve their personal and professional goals. These opportunities have enabled me to make the world a healthier place, and have provided ample dissemination and testing of what I call the Seven Laws of Achievement.

In addition to spreading the laws abroad, I am an avid supporter of many domestic organizations, many which are non-profit. I share my "laws" with them as well. Since 2007,

I have led or supported the construction of more than 50 Habitat for Humanity homes and served as a board director on a dozen civic organizations. I have also used the Seven Laws of Achievement as a foundation for the formal mentoring relationships that I have with numerous industry professionals. My "students" include general managers, site and team leaders, and vice presidents.

I do not have a patent on my success, and I willingly share it often with high school and university students, churches, corporations, and at-risk youths. With my faith as a foundation, I can trace every accomplishment of my life back to The Seven Laws of Achievement: Attitude, Ability, Aim, Active Practice, Adaptability, Association, and Accomplishment. It's not rocket science, but it can feel like it. Read carefully and with intent so that you can grasp and apply the principles contained in these pages. They will lead you towards your own personal road to success.

Why Read This Book?

Many books have been written about goals, achievement, and success. The library and internet are filled with thousands of self-help books on these topics, and their authors are all quite skilled at sharing their own methodologies. *The Seven Laws of Achievement* is a combination of life-acquired knowledge and firsthand experience.

The laws I present are the result of things that went as planned, but they also reflect things that did not go as planned. In this book I will take you through each of the seven laws, and you will see how they were formed. I certainly wasn't born with a silver spoon in my mouth, nor was there an inheritance or an influential family member or friend around to give me a head start. A more fitting description of my life before the seven laws is found in Langston Hughes' poem *Mother to Son*:

> *Well, son, I'll tell:*
> *Life for me ain't been no crystal stair.*
> *Its' had tacks in it.*
> *And splinters, and boards torn up,*
> *And places with no carpet on the floor –bare....*

I have shared this with you because it is very important that you make an active decision to read this book. Here are questions you should answer for yourself.

1. Is the knowledge and advice offered based on what the person experienced, or is it something they've read and never applied?

2. Is the advice applicable to me?

3. Is the advice applicable to my situation and to the present time?

Given what you have learned so far, I expect that you can answer "yes" to each of these questions. I would also like to assure you that The Seven Laws of Achievement are time and event tested. They are not bound to gender, generation, race, or nationality. They are applicable to any situation where a significant goal is desired and has presented a challenge. They are as applicable today as they were to me back in the late 1970s when I stumbled into them. They worked for me and will work for you too.

CONTENTS

CHAPTER 1

The Law of Attitude

"It is your attitude at the beginning of a task that determines success or failure."

– Corrine Dewlow

The first law of achievement rightfully starts with your attitude. It states: *The beginning of your success starts with how you think.* Webster defines attitude as: *a feeling of emotion toward a fact or state.* The foundation of every successful achievement must be a solid feeling or belief that the mountaintop will indeed be reached. This foundation must be rock solid and firm – otherwise it is not a foundation. It must stand strong and fast under all circumstances.

Why is this so? There is a saying that goes like this: regardless of your lot in life, you are either heading into a life storm, in a life storm, or coming out of a life storm. Your beliefs must be strong enough to endure each of these scenarios. A weak attitude (and thus a weak foundation) provides no more than a recipe for failure because setbacks and storms will constantly rear up. You must believe beyond a shadow of doubt that no matter how the wind blows, you will remain steadfast.

Achieving a positive attitude is not always intuitive. I

personally have not always had a positive attitude toward life or my ability to succeed. In my early teens, I faced a harsh reality as I watched my two older brothers struggle against the allure of drug and alcohol abuse. Their addictions shackled their God given gifts and talents and they were high school dropouts.

Similarly, although she did not struggle with drugs or alcohol, my older sister followed her brothers' lead and she also failed to procure her high school diploma. With this model before me, I came perilously close to accepting that it was just a matter of time before my feet would stumble down the same path. I had no tools to fight against such a fate and knew no one at the time who could convince me that my life would be any different.

However, I had something that my older siblings did not, and when the time came, I chose to listen to a message I received. One hot summer night, I lay in bed trying to fall asleep. My younger brother, with whom I shared a bed, was already asleep when a song came on the radio that would forever change my life . The song, *The Greatest Love*, written by jazz artist George Benson, seemed to speak directly to me. I listened intently. It was as if God himself had sent the message to me, and more than three decades later, the chorus remains my life theme:

> *"I decided long ago, never to walk in anyone's shadow. If I failed, if I succeed...at least I lived as I believed. No matter what they take from me, they can't take away my dignity."*

– The Greatest Love, George Benson

After hearing these words, I immediately sprang up. I wondered: "Is it my destiny to live the life of my siblings? Is it the simple matter of just choosing to be different that will make me different?"

I believe that God answered my prayers that night through my interpretation of the song. My very own questions enabled me to see that I did not have to accept my sibling's fate as my own. I could be different simply by choosing to be different. There and then I chose to adopt a new attitude; one that was positive and based on a future that would be far different than my present reality.

I drifted to sleep peacefully and awoke refreshed. While performing the morning ritual of washing my face and brushing my teeth, I stared back at the reflection that faced me in the bathroom mirror. I did this for a full 10 minutes – without blinking. I made a promise to myself, right then and there, to adopt and hold my new attitude and outlook on life – no matter what it had in store. As it turns out, my new attitude was actually grounded in more than just song.

The Theory Behind the Attitude

According to the Cognitive theory (Cameron & Green, 2011), our attitudes are directly linked to our values. Our values drive our belief system and our belief system impacts our attitudes. It's no secret that our attitudes are great predictors of our behavior and actions. The interesting fact is that our attitudes, which are anchored by our values, are not chosen for us at birth – we choose them. It doesn't matter whether you are rich, poor, black or white; you were not born with your values. You were not born with your attitudes, either. You develop them.

Similarly, as it is true that you can choose your values, it is also true that you can choose your attitude. Consider the connections I shared with my brothers: we were all born into the same family, we all had the same parents, and all went to the same schools, had the same teachers and pretty much experienced the same positive and negative life experiences. The key difference between my three older siblings and me is the simple fact that I adopted a different value system, which triggered a different attitude, which triggered different behaviors. I make no claim to be better than them in any shape, form, or fashion. I simply chose a different attitude.

Another interesting attribute of successful people is that they have an unwavering belief that they will be successful at whatever they attempt (Goldsmith, 2007). I remember like it was yesterday what happened to me right after I adopted my new value system, or my new attitude.

No, my situation at home did not change. I didn't know how or when I would be successful; I just knew that it would come. I now valued education and I had made a promise to myself. Almost immediately, my teachers noticed the change in me. My new belief system influenced my behavior and my approach to homework. My grades improved significantly. Where I had once been close to failing, I was soon enjoying an elite rank in the top 10 percent of students in my school.

That was just the beginning. On July 4th, 1978 (one year after first hearing that fateful George Benson ballad) I sat on the asphalted basketball court with a group of friends from the neighborhood. We had spent the entire day playing in the hot summer sun. In two months, we would all begin our last year of high school. With sweat dripping from our brows in the 90 degree heat, I took the opportunity to engage in a forward-thinking conversation that was representative of my optimistic outlook.

"Man, I can't believe that we are going into our last year of high school. It's going to be great when we are all successful adults," I said smiling.

"Yeah, I'm going to be a computer programmer," someone shouted.

"I'm going to be a banker," shouted another.

"I'm going to play for the Minnesota Vikings," was chimed in by my best friend Red.

Red was a starter on the high school football team and I believed, like many others, that he would indeed, most likely go on to play for the Vikings.

"Me, I'm going to be an engineer," I spoke last.

Red cracked up laughing. His outburst created a chorus of laughter. He knew all about my family – that my older brothers and sisters had been high school drop outs. He knew about the drugs. He knew about the financial struggles. To Red, I was just as likely to set foot on the moon as to go to college and become an engineer.

"I'll tell you what, I'll let you and your wife be my janitor while I'm playing for the Vikings," he carried on, causing everyone else to laugh just a bit louder.

With my back against the wall and still possessing a positive attitude, I issued a challenge to everyone sitting on that hot asphalt as the moon began to appear and the daylight to dwindle.

"Okay, here's what we'll do. We will all agree to meet back here in this same spot ten years from now when we have achieved these goals. Do we have a deal?" I somehow spoke bravely, all the while trying to silence the laughter with this bold dare.

Not one person backed away or expressed reluctance calling me on my statement. As a matter of fact, a round of high five hand slaps traveled our sitting circle indicating unanimous agreement. We agreed that in ten year's time, we would meet back in the same park at the same time on the same date.

On July 4th 1988 at 9pm I went back to the park as agreed. I was hopeful and anticipated a joyous reunion. My anticipation disappeared quickly when I discovered that I was the only soul on the court over the age of 12 (some neighborhood little kids now inhabited my old stomping ground). I waited for two hours, but no one ever showed up. I was the only one from the group that had achieved their stated goal. It was one of the saddest moments of my life. The odds against me were enormous, bigger than those of most others. For many years I wondered why I had been the only one who returned. Now, we all know the answer, it was my attitude.

What I had experienced on the court that day was what researchers call the cognitive dissonance theory. Cognitive dissonance refers to your belief that something is true even when there is great evidence that it may not be so. There was clear evidence that my goal to be an engineer should have never been realized, but my over-riding faith and positive attitude did not accept the evidence.

In the book, *The Choice is Yours: Today's Decisions for the Rest of Your Life*, John Maxwell (2005) concluded that more than any other factor, attitude has the greatest potential to determine what we get out of life. Looking back over that time, I have to admit I agree with Mr. Maxwell – 100 percent.

My First Job

Though I am now able to articulate exactly what a good attitude accomplished, I did have a few anxious moments along the way. Yet, I kept going forward. At age 19, I applied for my first engineering job. I was a second-semester freshman and a bit wet behind the ears. I had four years ahead of me before I would complete my engineering degree.

Needing money in the worst way, I tried to get a job in a co-op as an engineering intern, but was told by the career counseling office that I had to wait a full year before I could apply. These were considered to be plum jobs because they paid an average salary of $500 every two weeks (after taxes), but the school frowned on freshman working in the cooperative program. They preferred that students use their first two years to become adjusted to college life.

I, and many of my peers, interpreted this guidance to mean that the school did not believe freshman students were mature enough to handle the rigors of the corporate environment. My attitude and growling stomach disagreed on these points, so undeterred, I set out on a Monday morning determined to prove the academicians wrong.

I put on my best suit (a two-piece number that I bought at J C Penney) and walked into the first engineering firm that crossed my path in downtown Detroit. I took the elevator up to the tenth floor of a huge building and stepped out into my first real corporate America venture. Full of confidence, I opened a large wooden door that had the name of some company written on it and walked in toward a receptionist who sat in the center of a large waiting area.

In a polite manner, I asked if I could meet with the President of the firm. The receptionist asked me if I had an appointment, and I replied that I did not. Before she could point me in the direction of the door, I told her of my desire to work there and how I believed that I could be an asset to the firm. Impressed with my attitude, she asked me to take a seat, explaining as she walked away that she was going to check on the availability of said president.

Within minutes, a short man with the perfect haircut and a flashy smile emerged from an office, his right hand outstretched towards mine. He introduced himself as the president of the firm and I stood immediately to shake his hand. I told him my name and followed him back into his office. Once seated at his large paper-covered oak desk, I started into the five minute drill that I had rehearsed in my mind. The conversation went something like this:

"Let me get this right: you are still in your freshman year and you haven't taken a technical course yet. Is that correct?" he asked politely.

"That's right sir," I replied.

"Why should I hire you then," he queried.

With a confident look on my face, I smiled and responded: "Because I am confident that I can do whatever assignment you give me and I know that I'll be a great employee who will help your company grow."

An eerie silence filled the room. My interviewer sat back in his chair, and it almost felt as if he were looking straight through me.

That was it. The entire interview took every bit of ten

minutes, and in the end I was offered a job as an engineering technician. Having very little exposure to the engineering field at that time, I spent hours sitting at a drafting board designing anti-corrosive protection systems to be used at companies like General Motors, Chrysler and Ford. I carried forward, undisturbed, my positive attitude propelling me forward every day I was on that job, and I learned quickly. People around me helped me because of my attitude. I stayed there for two years before moving onto an engineering job at General Motors Detroit Diesel company. I am proof positive of what hiring professionals have noted. It is so hard to measure attitude that almost half of all people that are hired in organizations fail within 18 months (Caudron, 1997) and almost 90% of employees fail because of attitude issues, those who are correctly assessed as having, and who exhibit a proper attitude, do succeed. I was no exception.

Working it Forward, With Confidence and Feeling

Historically, professionals have given great credence to the importance of a good attitude. Human resource specialists are no exception here. Dr. Alan Davidson (Caudron, 1997), President of Psychological Consultants to Management, argued that people who have the right attitude are more likely to acquire the skills they need to do the job.

Numerous HR professionals believe that those with the right attitude are also more likely to learn new skills once on the job and to develop and progress more rapidly than those who struggle with a poor attitude. This theory is also backed by John Maxwell (2005), who posited that if two people are equal in talent, the winning edge will always go to the person with the right attitude. Over the years I myself have led numerous recruitment teams that hired hundreds of people to work in a variety of positions and I have found that putting this view into practice is rewarding. At the end of each interview session, I ask every interview panel one final question regarding their perspective of each person they interview:

> *"As things can and will sometimes get bad and gloomy in our business environment, do you believe that this individual possesses an attitude that they can use to help make things better?"*

If the answer was not a resounding, "yes," the candidates chances of gaining employment with my team decreased. Although technical skills were important, I sometimes placed equal – if not higher – value on the candidate's attitude. Thus, the majority of the work teams that I have assembled over the years have been based on an attitude-first and skill-second approach to hiring. The result has been a strong string of successful teams. Many who have begun in lower-level jobs have used their attitude to attain positions as general managers and vice presidents. Experience has proven that John Maxwell was right in arguing that people may not have control over the circumstances that may have placed them in their present situation, but that they always have the option to chose to have a good attitude and that living by this choice reaps rewards. There is one more aspect to this, and it completes our study of attitude.

David Niven, author of *100 Simple Secrets of Successful People* (2009) analyzed the results of hundreds of research studies that focused on achievement and the role that confidence plays. He concluded that a key attribute of successful people is that they believe in themselves more than others. Consider the words of Bible as a very early, yet timeless supporter of this:

> *As a man thinketh in his heart so is he*[ii].
>
> – Proverbs 23:7

In other words, a man will become what he believes. Another revelation in this passage that is worth noting is that the power of belief is greatest when it stems from the heart rather than from the brain. Why the heart? When people commit something to the brain, there is a good chance that obstacles can enter. However, when something is committed to the heart, a pack of wild dogs is needed to get through.

In other words, your head may fool you, but your heart will never lie. When you commit to something with your heart, your thoughts and actions will be driven by an attitude that is not easily swayed. In the book, *The Heart Has its Own Brain and Consciousness*, researchers Bradley, McCraty, and Tomasino (2012) concluded that the heart is a sensory organ that is actually capable of processing information. Research has even shown that the heart actually sends signals to the brain and that the heart can influence the brain's decision-making functions. This means that the heart knows what's going on long before your brain does.

A few years ago while living in Alabama I stumbled upon a baseball nestled in the red clay dirt outside of the homerun fence of the high school that was near my house. I picked up the ball and examined it closely. The slightly dented patch on one of its faces, and the location of the ball together were dead giveaways – this was probably a home-run, hit many moons ago.

Now, I'm not a baseball player, and you may not be either, but this was a major league sized park. Ask any pro and they will tell you that hitting a ball traveling at 90 miles per hour is one of the most difficult things any athlete ever does. It's so difficult that if you can hit a ball 3 out of 10 times, your performance is considered well above average, even among the pro ranks.

Whoever had hit that baseball out of the park probably had not approached home plate thinking that he would strike out. I believe that it was quite the opposite; he approached it believing in his heart that he would hit a home run. Of this I am certain.

Ten years later, the ball is still covered with the red stains that were impressed upon it when it settled in the Alabama dirt, and that covered it when I happened upon it. However, in addition to the red stain, it is now covered with positive quotes from the Bible and a host of world leaders. It sits under protective glass on my desk at work. Every morning before I start my day, I look at this baseball and remind myself of the importance of attitude. Inspiration can come from anywhere, and your good attitude will enable you to find it.

CHAPTER 2

The Law of Ability

The second law of achievement is the Law of Ability. It states that Everyone is born with their abilities untapped. One of life's great challenges that everyone must face is to locate the key that will unlock those innate abilities. Here's an example of what I'm referring to, from the middle of the movie Sister Act. For those of you who are not familiar, Sister Mary Clarence is a Las Vegas showgirl who witnesses a murder and is placed in protective custody by the police. A church, operated by nuns, becomes the perfect hiding place for Sister Mary Clarence while the police complete their investigation.

As the movie progresses, Sister Mary Clarence becomes a bit acclimated and forms relationships with some of the real nuns. One of them, Sister Mary Roberts, looks up to the newly-garbed nun one day and declares, "I've always felt that there is something inside of me that I've always wanted to give and that it's only for me to give." She is unable to name the feeling, but she knows she possesses a raw talent that is just bursting to come out. Later in the movie, when Whoopi's character really transforms into the role of choir director, she takes Sister Mary Roberts on and mentors her in the art of singing. All progresses well, but it takes a special event for Sister Mary Roberts to shine. This happens during a Sunday service. Sister Mary Roberts got a chance to unleash her voice for the first time as a soloist. In dramatic movie fashion, people start coming in off the streets to hear her powerful voice. She had discovered and unleashed her ability.

A Startling Statistic

During the 1990s I visited many Detroit middle and high schools. My goal was to inspire and motivate students to stay in school and complete a college education. I often began these workshops with a little challenge. I proposed to give five dollars to anyone who could answer the following simple question: *Where is the wealthiest place on earth?*

Before you read on, consider your answer. Now, I will tell you that most answers were a result of materialistic thinking. Students replied with answers like, "Oh, it's Fort Knox," or, "the local bank." Places such as Saudi Arabia andWashington, D.C. were often given.

Not one of the hundreds of students that I've challenged to answer this question years has arrived at the correct answer. As a matter of fact, they are usually shocked and silent when I tell them the wealthiest place on earth is the cemetery. According to Pastor Myles Munroe (1992), the cemetery is full of people who have died without recognizing or using their God-given abilities. Thus, their unique talents died with them.

Imagine if just a small percentage of these people had taken advantage of life's opportunities. Maybe one of them could have found the cure for cancer, AIDs, or the common cold,. Maybe today we would have cars that fly, planes that travel to planets and other technology that could improve our lives.

Don't be one of those people. Do not let your abilities die with you. Exploit them now. We all have capabilities that we do not use to full advantage. Why? First, because often we simply are unwilling to identify them. We are happy to go along doing what we do, and nothing more. Seek to identify your unique talents and the likelihood that you too will add to the wealth of this world increased dramatically. Don't "take it with you."

The Theory Behind Ability

Yes, the statements made in the previous section are bold. How are you supposed to go about unveiling something that is apparently hidden? By understanding your abilities. Here's a look at the science behind the Law of Ability.

Klausmeire and Ripple (1971) noted that we all have two specific types of abilities: cognitive and psychomotor. Cognitive abilities are those that allow us to think through, interact with, or interpret what happens around us. These are the abilities that we use, for example, when confronted with a directional sign flashing in front of you while traveling down the highway at 70 miles per hour. You have to interpret and react to the sign in mere seconds.

Psychomotor abilities are those that involve manual dexterity, such as: using tools, playing the piano, or swinging a baseball bat. According to Klausmeire and Ripple, everyone should assess whether their abilities are more prevalent in the cognitive or psychomotor sphere. Doing so provides an understanding of abilities, and this can lead to noticing and unleashing them.

In the summer issue of the journal, *Prenatal and Perinatal Psychology and Health*, Gino Soldera (2002) supports the conclusion that every person is born with innate abilities. He refers to these as the"Life Project." Every person's individual "Life Project" is programmed at conception and contains everything a person needs to fulfill his or her potential. This "Life Project" is actually resident within the DNA, according to Soldera.

No matter what you call it, what is referred to by myself, by the researchers Klausmeire, Ripple, and Soldera is defined as *"competence in an activity or occupation because of one's skill, training, or other occupation* (dictionary.com). Cognitive abilities may provide the ability to use our talents; psychomotor skills may enable us to benefit from training, but there must be something to work with for these to matter.

Every person has a natural genius embedded within them. The tragedy is that someone in our past – often a parent, a teacher, the media, or some other authority figure – convinced us to set aside our natural genius and encouraged us to pursue something quite different. The reasons given usually have something to do with money, with not becoming a dreamer, or with voicing that your genius is way off the beaten track.

Why is it, then, that we intellectually understand our abilities, but are still haunted as a species by the startling statistic you've read about (I'm referring to that cemetery full of talent). The reason is that facing challenges is tough. One of the most difficult ones that anyone will ever face is actually going back, tapping into your genius, and using it – in the face of repeated advice to the contrary. A real-life example of how a an individual tapped into his natural abilities will serve as a firm acknowledgment that it is indeed possible.

In college, I had a "special" acquaintance. His name was James, and he was a paraplegic. With his arms amputated at the elbow, he used two metallic extensions with hooks on each end that served as arms and fingers. His legs had been removed right at the torso. He maneuvered around campus in a powered wheelchair that he controlled with a joystick. That alone was amazing to me because he drove that chair deftly through several pretty tough Michigan snowstorms.

One day I saw James do something that forever changed my entire perspective. I was about to don my gym clothes when James rolled by. He rolled right up to me and stopped . I had never seen him the gym before, and I presumed he was cruising through and wanted to say a quick hello.

That's not exactly what happened. Attending to the task at

hand, I looked up and noticed James was holding a pair of swimming trunks. Slightly bemused, I was about to lace up my sneakers when I heard James ask if I could help him change into his swimming trunks. As uncomfortable as it was, I helped him undress and slipped a pair of trunks over his torso. He helped, laying still and flat out on the bench I had helped him get to. He looked like a baby who was about to have a diaper changed.

I was asked to remove James' mechanical arms. All set now, swim trunks on, he rolled over, landed on the ground and hobbled back up into his chair – unassisted. This was absolutely amazing!

I followed James out onto the deck that led to the pool. He pulled his chair up near the pool and, leaned over head-first and dove right into the water. I was ready to jump in and to save him. Within seconds, however, James was flat on his back, moving his armless stubs back and forth. To my surprise… he was swimming.

I watched James for about 30 minutes as he swam multiple laps back and forth along the length of the pool. I can remember each stroke, each lap, with clarity to this day. His amazing ability to swim with no legs and just stubs for arms come to my mind often. If he could do this, what could he not do?

My psyche is inflamed to this day when I think about James. If he could overcome what appeared to be an insurmountable physical disability, why couldn't I deal with the trivialities of everyday life? My answer has remained the same for decades, all owing to a conversation I had with James a few months after our swimming escapade. Summoning up more than all the courage I had, I asked James just how he was able to persevere and learn to do things such as swim the entire length of an Olympic-sized-pool. He looked at me and smiled before saying:"there is still ability in disability. I just had to change my approach until I found it."

It's All Inside

When I was 13 years old, the Adidas Company came out with the first pair of $100 sneakers. They were called "Top Ten" and every great basketball player wore a pair. Adidas basketball commercials were on every TV constantly, and really hit the forefront on Saturdays and Sundays during basketball season.

The Adidas marketing ploy was that if you had a pair of Top Ten sneakers, then you could acquire the abilities of great players like Kareem Abdul Jabbar or Rick Barry. In my junior year of high school, I worked every job I could find. I took out trash, raked yards, walked dogs; I did anything that I could find to make a dollar until I saved up and had 100 of them. I raced to the athletic store and quickly purchased the mythical shoes.

The next day, I stepped out on the court with my new Top Ten shoes; the glare of their shiny leather tops seeming to light up the black asphalt with every step I took. My friends bellowed oohs and ahhs. Although I had some ability to play the game, it didn't take long for me to realize that the shoes were mythical and not magical. My performance that day was no better than it had been any other day, pre-Top Ten. That day I learned firsthand that ability comes from the inside, not from the outside in.

CHAPTER 3

The Law of Aim

The third law of achievement is the Law of Aim. It states: *Aim for something big and you will not miss.* After setting a foundation based on a good strong attitude, and using your innate abilities, you can invoke this law to aim at desired goals. Goal setting can be difficult, but not if you aim with intent.

A goal is a dream with a timeline attached to it. In their book, *Goal Setting Among Adolescents: A Comparison of Delinquent, At-Risk, and Not At-Risk Youth*, Carroll, Durkin, Hattie, & Houghton, (1997) explain that goals trigger our behaviors. Whatever your position or place in life, you should aim your abilities toward a significant goal. What this means is that your abilities have no measurable value if you are not aiming them at something worth achieving.

As a youngster, I possessed a natural inclination for taking things apart. I just loved to figure out how electronic devices were put together and how they worked. I disassembled (much to the dismay of my family members) toasters, phones, radios, lamps, and anything else electrical that I could get my hands on. I became very good at this, but I was rarely able to put those things back together again. This didn't matter to me; the taking apart was the fun of it.

I didn't know it at the time, but my little hobby of busting up household appliances would eventually develop fully and blossom into a keen interest in engineering. With the help of a mentor, I accepted the challenge of growing and nurturing my technical abilities and took aim at the goal of achieving an electrical engineering degree. As I was just 14 years old at the time, I didn't know how or where I'd procure such an education, but I knew that I wanted it more than anything else. I studiously matriculated from high school, went off to college, and five years later graduated with a degree in electrical and computer engineering. The electrical design skills I had refined were instrumental in meeting the needs of consumers in the automotive, chemical, and food industries.

Lessons Learned

Thinking back on these experiences, (including Jack) – and on my reaction to them – I was intrigued many years later when I came across an article in *Success* magazine in (October, 2009) that featured interviews with Brian Tracey and Cynthia Kersey. The words of these motivational businesspeople focused on two basic tenets, and I have learned those two lessons well.

First, goals should be written down. Brian Tracey argued that people should not only write the goal down, but they should make a list of everything that will have to be done to achieve it. Furthermore, he suggested prioritizing the list and then organizing it sequentially to facilitate understanding of what resources will be needed at each step along the way.

Though this may sound quite prescriptive and disciplined, it is a sound approach and it does work. Today, I facilitate global engineering solutions that net millions of dollars to my employer. This involves influencing and motivating the human talent from countries with a great variety of native languages and cultures. Before starting any capital intensive activity, I work together with the people who need to understand the goals. These are drafted with timelines of what will be done by whom and at what cost. I also use this approach with personal goals and now have a great habit that really enables me to achieve what I set out to do.

The second lesson I gleaned from those same interviews is that it is important to understand and be aware of the role that fear and self-doubt play in goal setting and achievement. Tracey argued that fear of failure can be so great that it can actually prevent people from even attempting to achieve something of significance.

Fear is the opposite of faith, and it is faith that will overcome self-doubt. Here is what the Bible (Matthew 17:20) has to say on the matter: **"I tell you the truth, if you have faith as small as a mustard seed, you can say to this mountain, 'Move from here to there' and it will move."** An important fact about the relationship between the two powers of fear and faith: it is impossible to have both equally at the same time in the same place. You will either have more of one or the other. The good news is that the smallest amount of faith is usually enough to achieve success.

While faith can move mountains, fear undermines it by chipping away at it bit by bit, every day, in every way. Therefore, goals have to be fed a daily dose of faith or they are subject to becoming undermined by fear. For the record, I've had my share of failures – too many to count. As a matter of fact, I've not only had my share, but I think I've also had someone else's share as well.

Failure

Sometimes, it is not fear that stops you. There are numerous things that can get in the way of our goals, or cause them to change. That said, I never let a failure define me as a person. Zig Ziglar said it best, "failure is an event, not a person." Business and management authors Wilson and Dobson (2008) emphasized in their book, *Goal Setting: How to Create an Action Plan and Achieve Your Goals,* that people who work hard at avoiding failure actually miss the adventure of personal growth. I agree wholeheartedly; many of the best life lessons for me did not come from my successes, they came from my failures. To support his argument that failure is a part of our learning process, FBI instructor Gregory Milonovich (2011) shared an approach that he uses to learn from failed attempts. He called it the RADICAL approach. Radical is an acronym that means:

Review	Review what happened in detail.
Analyze	Dissect the event for better understanding.
Diagnose	Identify the root cause of the event.
Independent source.	Seek to confirm the cause with an objective
Candid	Don't sugarcoat; be honest with the assessment.
Accountability you.	Accept where the finger points, even if it's at
Learn	Agree on what can better done better next time.

In high school, I often ran the 880 yard race. I never finished a race above third place. I'd start every race, fully aware of my abilities (at least I thought I did at the time) and full of self-confidence. At the sound of the gun I was always first to jump out front. At the first curve, someone would normally run past me, despite my best effort to maintain my lead.

However, between the first and the second curve I stayed right on the heel of the leader and tried to match him step for step. My second place position felt secure and I believed that by matching the leader's pace I was guaranteed at least a second place finish. At the third curve, the first set of feet of an opponent from the rear usually ran past me. At this point I'm now watching and trying to match the pace of the two runners ahead of me.

By the time I got to the fourth curve, two or more runners were normally past me. At that moment, I would run frantically trying to match pace with the leader and everyone else ahead of me. By the time we got to the last lap, I was so confused and out of breath from trying to keep up with everyone that that I just gave up. Every race ended the same way, as I tried to focus on making it past the mythical big rock that sat near the edge of the track and was alleged to have cursed many runners. Even though everyone had to run past the rock, it seemed like the cursed rock impacted me more than anyone else. By the time I got to the finish line, the winner had already left the track and was heartily celebrating the achievement of his goal, while I usually fell to the track's rubberized surface catching my breath and deeply lamenting my failure.

In his book, *18 Minutes: Find Your Focus, Master Distractions, and Get the Right Things Done*, Peter Bregman (2011) noted that most people will exert significant energy and effort to avoid failures. He argued that performance improvement may stall if we don't risk failing. Referencing the extensive research conducted by Dr. Carol Dweck, professor at Stanford University, Bregman highlighted the risk of believing that talent is fixed. Bregman emphasized that people that ascribe to the myth that talent is fixed believe that failure illuminates their limit and they will go to extremes to avoid the limit. Several years ago, Nike ran a Michael Jordan commercial that best captured the mindset that we should have when faced with falling short of achieving goals. Looking into the camera, Michael said:

> *"I've missed more than 9000 shots in my career.*
> *I've lost almost 300 games. Twenty six times I've*

been trusted to take the game winning shot and missed. I've failed over and over again in my life. And that is why I succeed."

It's been 30 years since my last race, but the many race failures still stand as constant reminders of Zig's golden rule... failure is an event and not a person.

Locke, Shaw, Saari and Latham (1980) affirmed that setting goals is an effective tool to achieve success. Their research concluded that performance is enhanced when goals are present. Their research showed that that there is a correlation between specific and challenging goals and higher performance. According to the researchers, goals affect performance by directing attention, mobilizing effort, increasing persistence, and motivating strategy development. If you define your goal as simply "doing your best," you are actually setting no goal at all. Goals must be specific and focused.

Two triggers that can make the difference between having a challenging goal and no goals at all are self awareness and self confidence. According to Locke (and others), by being self-aware of our strengths and weaknesses we get a feel for just how far our abilities can take us. With self confidence we demonstrate just how much trust we have in our abilities to achieve our goals. For instance, long before I entered my first engineering lecture, I was aware that I possessed abilities to engage others. I also had confidence that my abilities would propel me toward my goal of attaining my

BS in electrical engineering.

There are two types of goals: mastery and performance (Dweck, 1988). Mastery goals are used to acquire a new skill or enhance an existing one. Performance goals are focused on demonstrating a skill.

Your discovered ability will point you toward the type of goal with which you should align yourself. If you are focused on an athletic ability, your goal may be a performance goal. If you are focused on playing the piano, you may want to target a mastery goal. This does not mean that playing basketball can't include mastery goal or that playing the piano can't have a demonstration goal. The key here is to know the type of goal that will best lead you where you are trying to go.

CHAPTER 4

Law of Active Practice

The fourth law of achievement is the Law of Action. It states that: *abilities come by birth, but mastery comes by practice.* Once you have a great attitude, know your abilities, and have identified a proper set of goals, it is time to swing into action.

During the winter semester of fifth grade, many of the boys in my neighborhood took out a membership at a neighborhood gymnasium that was operated by the city police department. The intent of those who sponsored this gymnasium was to provide urban youth an alternative to hanging out in the streets. One day, my best friend and I went to this gym together, and he challenged me to a game of one-on-one basketball. Although I thought I was the better athlete, he won the game by a score of 15 to 10. My ego was crushed by the loss.

A week passed and I was unable to shake the debilitating feelings of failure that accompanied that loss. This would not do, so I decided I had only one choice. I needed to improve. However, coaching cost money, and that was in short supply. As chance would have it, a solution came in the form of a candy sale. I participated in a school candy drive and sold enough Jolly Ranchers over the next month to win the company's competition. First place rewarded a basketball.

Armed with my very own ball, I practiced every day after school. If the neighborhood court was vacant, I practiced shooting there. If the court was full, I practiced dribbling the ball down the street. I didn't count, but I'm sure I logged a thousand hours of practice.

A few months later, I challenged that best friend to a rematch game. He had no idea that I had spent hours honing my skills and pouring everything I had into my game. I won the game 15-6. The difference can be boiled down to one important attribute that my friend knew all about but that I did not – practice. In the movie, The Wizard of Oz, the Lion gives a memorable sermon about the power of a missing attribute.

> *Courage! What makes a king out of a slave? Courage! What makes the flag on the mast to wave? Courage! What makes the elephant charge his tusk in the misty mist, or the dusky dusk? What makes the muskrat guard his musk? Courage! What makes the sphinx the seventh wonder? Courage! What makes the dawn come up like thunder? Courage! What makes the Hottentot so hot? What puts the "ape" in apricot? What have they got that I ain't got?*
>
> Dorothy, Scarecrow, Tin Woodsman: Courage!

Kathleen Cushman, author of the book *Fires in the Mind: What Kids Can Tell Us About Mastery and Motivation*, and founder of the non-profit organization What Kids Can Do, noted that cognitive research has proven that that it takes about 10000 hours of practice to become good at what we do (Cushman, 2010). Most people think that exceptional athletes likeTiger Woods and Michael Jordan are simply born with the talent to play their respective sports at an exceptional level. It may be true that they were born with talent, but their excellence was a direct result of thousands of hours of practice.

Similarly, Malcolm Gladwell, author of the book *Outliers: The Story of Success* (2008), cited research that was conducted about violin players in Germany. The researchers catalogued the number of hours that student violinists spent practicing during three stages of their lives: childhood, adolescence, and adulthood. After analyzing the results, the researchers concluded that: the violinists that were considered stars logged 10,000 or more hours of practice; those that were considered good performers practiced for 8000 hours; and, those that were considered future teacher musicians logged 4000 hours. Active practice made a big difference in terms of performance results.

We are all born with a talent of some sort, but no one is born with skill or mastery. It takes practice to turn a talent into a skill. That's what Daniel Coyle learned after analyzing more than three dozen research studies on talent conducted between 1965 and 2008. He summarized his findings in his book, *The Talent Code*, concluding that ordinary people can achieve significant results simply by logging hours of practice.

What does this mean? If your goal is to be a writer, you need keep practicing your writing. If you goal is to be an engineer, keep drilling in math and science, and actively practice the tools of your discipline. Whatever the goal, the odds are in your favor that you will be successful if you practice.

Make Action a Habit

University of London researchers Lally, Potts, Wardle, and Van Jaardsveld (2010), argued in the July 2010 issue of the *European Journal of Psychology* that the hardest step toward achievement of a goal is the first step. This first step is also the one that requires the most planning. Thereafter, successive steps are undertaken using what has been learned. The more you know to begin, the easiest each of these steps will be.

There is more to it than that. The more you repeat an action, the less thought you have to put into your ultimate goal. To clarify, the ultimate goal is for the action – or doing it superbly – to become a habit. In fact, habit formation is the beginning of mastery. The question then becomes: How long does it takes to form a habit?

To answer this question, Lally (et al.) studied a group of 96 individuals. The purpose of the research was to identify the point at which an activity that is actively practiced becomes a habit. The participant group was asked to select an eating, drinking or some other simple behavior of their choice. The only criteria for the selection was it had to be something the participants were not presently engaged in. For example, some of the participants decided to take up meditation while others substituted junk food with healthy snacks. Analysis of the study result indicated that habits were formed on average within 66 days if the participant regularly practiced the activity. Mapping the results, the researched concluded that habit formation occurred on an asymptotic curve. An asymptotic curve is a curve that eventually plateaus and extends towards infinity. According to the researchers, habit formation occurred at the point on the graph where the ascent levels off.

Of particular note was the observation that half of the participants failed to reach the habit stage because they failed the consistency requirements. There are two significant results from this study: (1) what we do (and how frequently) impacts our habits, and (2) our habits determine whether or not we achieve our goals. The secret to achieving mastery is to practice an activity with enough consistency that it becomes a habit.

I attended high school in Michigan. One year our basketball team happened to compete against a high school in Lansing. The school, Everett High, had a player on it who would later become internationally famous. At the time, his abilities were incredible, and my school got trounced. I can't remember how many points he scored against our school, Union High, but it seemed like it was more than 50. Who was this player? His name was Earvin Johnson.

The sports writers wrote endlessly about this game, and about Earvin's natural skills. Years later, now known only as Magic (Johnson), he revealed his secret. His skills weren't natural; they were the result of years of hard and active practice. He played basketball every day. I don't mean he spent a little time at it. I mean he drilled, sweated and practiced day in and day out, 7 days a week, 52 weeks a year.

Unlike most Southern states, Michiganders switched sports as the seasons changed. In the Spring and Summer it was track and field, and basketball. In the Fall it was football and in the Winter it was hockey and wrestling. Magic was focused on his sport, and he played it year round, forsaking all others. He once told a story about how in the middle of winter he grabbed his basketball and a shovel and headed to a nearby court to practice. If you've ever experienced a Michigan winter, you know that practicing basketball outside in the cold requires dedication. There are three lessons that come to mind that are worth remembering about the importance of the law of active practice: (1) practice, (2) practice, and (3) practice.

CHAPTER 5

Law of Adaptability

Let's review our progress so far. We've got the right attitude. We've discovered our abilities and focused (or aimed) them on a goal. We keep a consistent and regular schedule and practice our abilities so that they become habitual.

We're now ready to take another step forward, using the fifth law of Achievement. This is the Law of Adaptability and it states that: *goals themselves may not change, but the path to them frequently will.*

Here's an example. I have a daily goal that may seem quite simple. It is to get to my office by 7:30 in the morning. I usually leave my house at 6:45 a.m. for the 45 minute commute down I-78. Doing the math, the goal of completing the trip in the time allotted seems attainable. However, things happen. Sometimes there are traffic jams. Sometimes roads are closed or there are detours. I may have to change lanes (taking me out of my middle lane comfort zone) and I may have to get off of I-78 altogether and take a different route. There may even be times when I have to give up on driving and take the train. I make these adjustments to reach my goal of getting to the office by 7:30. Notice that my goal never changed, it is just that the method of attaining it did. I had to adapt to changes in my environment and adjust my path. This is the basis of adaptability.

Adaptability in Practice

Successful people have a knack for constantly monitoring their performance relative to their goal and adjust as necessary. They check for obstacles by looking ahead. When they have free blocks of time, they do something that is in alignment with their goal. For instance, if they are trying to climb up the corporate ladder, they may spend time reading about their company, its products or services, or honing their skills. If the goal is to become or remain healthy, they may engage in a little exercise instead of watching TV.

Here's the story of a woman (a dear friend) who adapted beyond what most would be able to even visualize. Her name is Diane, and I first met her when while attending college. I was a junior and she was a recent graduate working for Ford Motor Company designing trucks.

What makes Diane's story inspirational is that her goal – according to stereotypical thinking, – should have never been achieved. At age sixteen, Diane got pregnant, became a teen mother and dropped out of high school. By the time she was 20 she had delivered three more children, and still had no education. Yet, she had set a goal for herself before all these things happened. She wanted to become an engineer.

Thus, at the age of 21, Diane enrolled in night school to

complete her GED. After obtaining it, she enrolled in Wayne County Community College, and graduated with a two-year degree. Still, she was not done. She transferred to my alma mater, Wayne State and after another two years, proudly walked across the stage in Cobo Arena to receive a degree in mechanical engineering. Diane could have stopped at the first obstacle, giving birth at 16 years of age, but she didn't. She could have stopped at the second or third child, but she didn't. In fact, it was a year after the birth of her third child that she decided that it was time to continue the pursuit of her dream of becoming an engineer. Five years passed since she had dropped out of high school, but she never lost sight of her goal. She had to adapt to a different path than what she might have envisioned before becoming pregnant with her first child, but she kept her goal in sight nonetheless. Although I haven't had contact with Diane in 10 years, I'll always remember her as living proof that the fifth law of achievement can work for anyone. It's not always a matter of how fast you get where you want to be. More often, it is simply refusing to veer off course.

Change like this does not come without psychological impact. After all, change means something different will happen, and humans are creatures of habit. Researcher and MIT professor Edgar Schein wrote in his book, *Organizational Culture and Leadership*, that two forces are present with each change we face. He called one force learning anxiety, and the other survival anxiety. Learning anxiety is spawned from the fear of learning something. It occurs because possible failure, as well as enhanced exposure, can creep in with every new turn. Schein argued that survival anxiety surfaces when we are left with a choice that is delivered by our natural instinct to survive. However, the selection of the choice is normally accompanied by negative thoughts such as the fear of being left behind or considered inferior if we are unable to adapt to change in an effective fashion.

In addition to anxiety, Schein concluded that the two anxieties, learning and survival, often expand into four different types of fear (Cameron & Green, 2011). The first is the fear of temporary incompetence. Here, we worry that we will not have the skills necessary to operate within the new environment that is brought about by a change. This inflicts quite a heavy blow to our self confidence. Expanding a bit on Diane's story, she at one point explained that her biggest fear regarding being both a teenage parent and student was that she would lose the academic focus that was required to survive the curriculum that included daily homework. She felt it was easier to walk away from the fear of failing high school than to face the challenge head on.

The second is the fear of punishment. Diane feared that the loss of her dream of being an engineer would be the punishment for getting pregnant in high school. That fear forced her to drop out of high school.

Third is the fear of loss of personal identity. Schein noted that internal struggles are created when a change alters our "habits or ways of thinking." In 1998, while working as unit operations manager in South Carolina, a forty-year employee informed me of his decision to retire. He had dedicated two-thirds of his life to the company and habitually arrived at work like clockwork on every scheduled workday. The only exceptions were vacation and sick days. When asked what he planned to do on the first day of his retirement he replied, "Sleep." After four weeks of "sleeping," the retiree called me up and asked if he could have his old job back. He confessed that he wasn't ready for the change and that working in the job gave him a personal sense of identity. Eventually, he overcame the fear of losing his identity by creating a new sense of personal identity as a volunteer at the local fire station.

Lastly, we are susceptible to the fear of loss of group membership when faced with change. Right or wrong, we gain societal identity through predictable habits and behaviors. According to Diane, the teen pregnancy forced her to grow up faster than the girls in her immediate peer group and the fear of losing that group identity made it difficult for her to participate in the normal things that usually define the American teenage demographic.

I can empathize. Five years into my career, I was offered a promotion that would take me away from the state of my birth for the first time. At this point, my world was defined by a large group of family and friends. The promotion was attractive to me in so many ways, but the fear of losing my group membership was so intense that I contemplated turning the offer down.

Three decades and more than a dozen different jobs (and promotions later, I've overcome the fear of change and learned to adapt. So, what was my secret? It was actually a "who," not a "what." Her name was Mrs. Twiggs, and she was a grand old lady that I knew from my hometown of Grand Rapids, Michigan. I first met her the day she retired from life as a housekeeper in 1979. She was a native Southerner and eventually migrated North, doing small lot jobs that included everything from seamstress to light factory manufacturing. On the day that she retired I rode past her house and saw her sitting on her porch. I stopped, expressed my congratulations at her retirement, and asked what her plans were.

"I'm going to be a fifth grade school teacher," she confidently asserted.

I smiled and continued riding my bike, thinking that she was just kidding and politely creating small talk. However, she was serious. At 60 years of age, and lacking a high school education, she started pursuing her lifelong goal of becoming an elementary school teacher. She started by attending night school, and a year later she earned her GED. She then enrolled in the local community college and earned an Associate's degree in education. Still on the path of her goal, at the age of 64, Mrs. Twiggs enrolled in a four year university. Building on the credits earned from her two year degree, she emerged two years later with a degree in elementary education. Finally, nearing 70 years of age, Mrs. Twiggs started teaching fifth graders.

In 1994, I ran into Mrs. Twiggs at my brother's wedding. I had told her inspiring story many times and just couldn't help myself. She was sitting in the church pew in front of me, and I couldn't resist telling her amazing story to the person sitting next to me. When I finished, I tapped Mrs. Twiggs on the shoulder and asked her to extend her right hand. As she did so, I noticed the glean on her 80 year old hand of a gold college ring that was loosely resting at the end of her index finger.

Though Mrs. Twiggs passed away years ago, the memory of her remarkable achievement stands as a perfect example of the law of adaptability. Her dream of becoming a teacher was about 50 years old when it came to fruition. If she can do it, so can you. After all, *goals may not change, but the path to them will change frequently.*

CHAPTER 6

Law of Association

The sixth law of achievement is the Law of Association. It postulates that *association impacts aspiration.*

"I wished my son had spent more time with you." Those words – spoken by the mother of my best childhood friend, Chuck – haunt me to this day. As a youngster, Chuck had been arrested a multitude of times, drank alcohol excessively, and indulged heavily in drugs. I admit that I found myself, more often than I care to remember, in the middle of some juvenile antics with Chuck. Though not drug or alcohol related, many had danger written all over them.

Truthfully, however, most of the incidents were created and executed by Chuck. I was the voice of reason and often talked him out of doing something that in the eyes of our parents or the legal system would have been labeled b-a-d with a capital B. Eventually I became so concerned that the repeated infractions would have a negative impact on my future that I chose to break off our friendship.

The revelation that Chuck was the source of his own troubles came to his mother years after I had graduated from college and long after the childhood escapades. However, they did come, and her unforgettable words serve as a reminder that we can make or break ourselves based on our choices.

Let's see how this fits by reviewing our mastery of the first five laws up to this point. One: you have a great attitude regarding your future. Two, you've discovered that you have many abilities that are loaded with potential for success. Three, you have set significant goals for yourself. Four, you are actively and consistently practicing your abilities in order to achieve mastery. Five, you are managing daily distractions that threaten to push your progress off track.

This law of association must be understood properly. Many people, when hearing "law of association," think about simple math and multiplication. In that arena, it doesn't matter how components (numbers) are grouped. The result of an action (multiplication or addition) will always be the same.

Yes, this works for math, but it does not work for achievement. It matters a great deal how you group, or associate, with others.

Although never validated by academic researchers, the "crabs in a barrel theory" has circulated within the Black community for years. Its general hypothesis is the basis of the sixth law of achievement. The theory goes like this: if you place crabs in a pot of boiling water, the crabs will seek to climb out. However, the moment one of the crabs is about to climb out, another crab will pull it back into the boiling water to prevent it from escaping. The moral of the story is that not everyone that you are associated with wants to see you achieve success.

Sometimes, even those who don the label of "friend" can be a crab in camouflage,. They are just waiting to rain on your parade and pull you back down. Like slick marketing campaigns that get you to buy something when you don' need it, these "friends" (or associates) can convince you to buy into thinking that your goals are impossible and that you should just give up and fall back into the barrel with them.

When I was trying to climb out of the barrel I was in, it wasn't my pessimistic views that threatened my climb. Rather, it was the pessimistic views of others around me. I can still hear faint claims like: "You won't last one day in Detroit" or "you'll be back home in a body bag," or even, "No one in your family has ever done anything like this, why do you have to be so different?" These words did not originate from enemies, People who were close to me made these statements. They were right in that I did see a dead person in a body bag and during my first two years in Detroit, I did have no fewer than three loaded guns aimed at my head. However, what they said was right for the wrong reason. They were not concerned for my safety and life progression, they simply wanted to discourage me from leaving and moving ahead.

In his book, *Learned Optimism*, Professor Martin Seligman, argued that anyone can be successful by adopting an optimistic outlook to "refashion" the negative things that happen and to reverse the powerful impact of pessimistic views that we place on ourselves (or those that others seek to place on us). Did you fail a test? Seligman argued that if so, it's not because you didn't prepare, it's because you believed that you were stupid. Did you get turned down for a date, he asked. Don't bother asking someone else because you believed that you were unlovable.

Discouragement can originate \from people who are close to you, from yourself, and from those in your peripheral environment. A pastor of a church I attended years ago once told me the following story. A chicken farmer went hiking in the hills near his farm one day and stumbled upon a strange looking egg. The egg was much larger than the small chicken eggs he was accustomed to. He picked the egg up, headed back to his farm, and placed the large egg into an incubator with other chicken eggs. As time went by, the large egg hatched a large bird. The farmer didn't know what to call the bird so he called it a chicken (like he called all the others). He raised the bird in the midst of all of the other chickens and every day he fed the bird nothing but chicken feed, until one day the bird began to act and think like a chicken. One day a stranger walked by the farm and saw the large bird walking and acting like a chicken. Puzzled, he stopped and asked the farmer, "Why are you raising that eagle among your chickens?" The farmer replied, "Eagle? Why that's no eagle, that's a chicken. All his life he has lived with other chickens, eaten nothing but chicken feed, and a chicken is all that he will ever be."

Many people are in a similar situation – they are an eagle raised among chickens and eating chicken feed. However, the chicken feed that they are eating takes the form of comments like "you'll never amount to anything good, you'll never succeed, why don't you just give up and come back to what the rest of us are doing", or (my personal favorite) "do you think you are better than the rest of us". These comments, although projected without the intent to harm, are all around us in subtle forms. They are on banners outside neighborhood stores that promote 40 ounce liquor for $1. They are on advertisement placards at bus stops that promote partying while you are heading off to work. They are the commercials that encourage children to spend $300 on a pair of sneakers rather than $20 on a book. The one that won the prize for me was two side-by-side billboards outside a fifth grade elementary school. One showed a picture of a bottle of bleach with a hypodermic needle in it and the message "clean before you use." The other was a roll of condoms fashioned to look like a roll of lifesavers candy. It doesn't take a rocket scientist to figure out the subliminal message that is delivered to the impressionable children that leave that school every day.

Another, and arguably the best example of the power of association was told to me by my friend Tony. Tony has a PhD and works for an automotive company in Detroit. Back in the 1930s a young boy walked past a store front window and saw a tweed hat in a display window. The display had quite a persuasive placard next to it that described the extraordinary qualities of the cap. The boy was so sold on the hat and its amazing qualities that he made up his mind that he would somehow get it. He worked every job he could find for weeks until he saved up the ten dollars that he needed. With his pockets and savings depleted, he placed the hat on his head, cocked it slightly to the side and walked home. He strutted through the door and immediately ran to his father to show him the new cap, fully expecting to be showered with praise and admiration.

"Dad, look at this sharp hat I just bought. What do you think?" he said modeling the fabric that sat on his head.

"How much did you pay for that?" his father asked.

"It took every penny of the ten dollars that I saved, but it was worth it," he beamed.

His father lowered the rim of his glasses, folded his arms and exhaled. He turned so that his son could not see the disappointment on his face and mumbled nine words loud enough for his son to hear. "A ten dollar hat on a ten cent head." He walked away.

It's all about the power of persuasion, and your associations determine what you are exposed to. Do not let just anyone or anything (like a $10 hat) choose you. You make the choice. Select it, value it, cherish it, and constantly check to make sure it serves you well.

CHAPTER 7

The Law of Accomplishment

The seventh (and final) law of achievement is called The Law of Accomplishment, and it states that *Success will last longest when it is given away.*

Before exploring this, take a moment to cement the idea in your memory that the seven laws are progressive. You must begin by understanding the first law and then proceed progressively through the others. This is not to say that it is impossible to achieve success without going through each step sequentially. of the world is full of successful people who have anomalously achieved success despite skipping a law or two. However, of the preponderance who do so are unable to sustain their success and they rarely surpass their expectations.

These laws were formed on a solid foundation of years of actual experience. The lessons learned during this continuing journey indicate that:

1. If you follow these laws, there is a very good chance that you will be successful. The confidence that you will enjoy as you master even the smallest of steps will be a guiding light illuminating the truth that success is not just a matter of choice, but a matter of

time.

2. Success will come when you run your own race. The key is to be ready when opportunity presents itself. For example, in the Bible Ecclesiastes 9:11 you'll find the following:

> *"I returned, and saw under the sun, that the race Is not to the swift, nor the battle to the strong, neither yet bread to the wise, nor yet riches to men of understanding, nor yet favor to men of skill."*

This is where most people stop on this scripture and many fail to read the powerful anchor of this scripture. It really drives home the point that achievement and success is available to everyone. The last sentence of the scripture makes the point:

> *"but time and chance happenth to them all."*

What does this mean? It means that you don't have to be the fastest to be successful. You don't have to be the strongest, you don't have to be the wisest, and you don't have to be the recipient of favors from others. Success comes to those who are ready when time and opportunity intersect. By working the through the seven laws of achievement you ensure that you are ready at this juncture.

3. What you do after you achieve success is just as important as what you did to achieve it. It is natural to sit back and enjoy the view afforded you from the mountaintop of your success. However, don't get

stuck on the mountaintop. Keep looking around.

Remember, life is lived on an incline; you will either move up or slide down. It is impossible to stay where you are. Always look forward to your next goal.

Give it Away

In the movie *Pay it Forward*, a young boy played by Haley Joel Osment starts a class project to make the world better by doing something nice for someone who does not expect it. He encourages others to join him. The idea is that if enough people keep the chain going of helping other people, significant change can be brought about. This can extend beyond a circle of friends to a neighborhood, an entire community, a city – the possibilities are actually endless.

I personally am standing on the shoulders of many people (alive and dead). I can never pay them back but I can actively seek opportunities to extend favor to those who similarly may never be able to return the gesture. Even simple deeds can produce amazing results.

Here's an example. In 1996, spoke to a group of 60 women in a correctional facility, sharing freely the benefits of my years of experience with these laws that you have learned. I also took time to remind them that although their bodies were incarcerated, their minds were still free. A week after the "visit," 1 I received 60 letters in the mail, one from each incarcerated person, explaining in detail the wrong that they had done in their lives and the right that they were going to do going forward. I still have each and every one of those letters.

I have found that the more I give of myself, the more others do the same. There is simply no better way to achieve true success – which I define as happiness – than to do unto others.

CHAPTER 8

Conclusion

Throughout these pages, you have learned how to achieve your heart's desire. However, a brief look at what our real needs are will provide enlightenment here. According to Maslow's Hierarchy of Needs, that every human being requires the following:

4. Food;

5. Security;

6. Love;

7. Esteem; and,

8. Self actualization.

These needs are progressive and prioritized. In other words, food is the most basic of our needs. After food, we focus on keeping a roof over our heads. Once we have a roof over our heads, we begin to look for love. Once we are satisfied that we are loved, we shift our efforts to building up our self esteem. Finally, after we are full, safe, loved, and optimistic about our place we life, we start to think about why we are on earth and what our higher purpose is.

The seven laws of achievement are very similar to the

hierarchy of needs. They are progressive, as each level must be completed before moving on to the next. Just as food feeds the body, attitude feeds the brain. Just as security has the potential to keep us safe, ability can be used to provide life choices that keep us safe. Love and aim are both choices that drive the way we behave. The confidence that is described by Maslow as need for esteem is the same confidence that comes from active practice and adaptability. Finally, just as self actualization causes a person to think about their purpose and impact on others, so do associations and accomplishment; they require knowing your position and giving thought of where you want to be. Most importantly, like self-actualization, the law of accomplishment requires that we relinquish sole proprietorship of our achievement and engage in the highest act of human kindness: sharing it with someone in need.

The Seven Laws of Achievement are not magical or mystical. They are free to everyone but you must commit to them. They will take you places that you've only visited in your dreams. You may find yourself sharing your ideas with CEO's or even a president of the United States. You may create an organization that makes the lives of other people better. You may pay it forward in foreign countries, or you may find fulfillment in your own back yard. You may even write books, like this one, which I hope has provided guidance and inspiration. Here's to your success and happiness.

References

Bregman, P. (2011). *18 Minutes: Find Your Focus, Master Distraction, and Get the Right Things Done.* New York, NY: Hachette Book Group.

Bradley, T. M. (2012). *The Heart Has its Own Brain and Consciousness.* Retrieved from Mindful Muscle: http://www.davidicke.com/headlines/72995-the-heart-has-its-own-brain-and-consciousness.

Cameron, E. C. & Green, M. (2011). *Making Sense of Change Management: A Complete Guide to Models, Tools, and Techniques of Organizational Change.* Great Britain: Kogan Page.

Carroll, A. A., Durkin, K. K., Hattie, J. J., & Houghton, S. S. (1997). Goal Setting Among Adolescents: A Comparison of Delinquent, At-Risk, and Not At-Risk Youth. *Journal Of Educational Psychology, 89*(3), 441-450.

Caudron, S. (1997). Hire for Attitude: Its Who They are that Counts. *Workforce-Costa Mesa,* 20-26.

Cushman, K. (2010). *Fires in The Mind:What Kids Can Tell Us About Mastery and Motivation.* San Francisco: Wiley.

Dobson, M. &. Wilson, S.B. (2008). *Goal Setting: How to Create an Action Plan and Achieve Your Goals.* New York: Amacom.

Dweck, C. (1988). Goals: An Approach to Motivation and Achievement. *Journal of Personality and Social Psychology,* 5-12.

Gladwell, M. (2008). Outliers: *The Story of Success.* New York, NY: Hachette Book Group.

Goldsmith, M. (2007). *What Got You Here Won't Get You There: How Successful People Become Even More Successful.* New York: Hyperion.

Klausmeire, H. &. (1971). *Learning and Human Abilities: Educational Psychology.* New York: Harper and Row.

Lally, P. Potts, H.W.W., Wardel, J., & Van Jaarsveld,C.H.M. (2010). How are Habits Formed: Modeling Habit Formation in the Real World. *European Journal of Psycology*, July, 2010, 998-1009.

Locke, E. A,Latham, G.P., Saari, K.N., Shaw,L.M. (1980). *Goal Setting and Task Performance.* Retrieved from Questia: www.Questia.com.

Maxwell, J. (2005). *The Choice is Yours: Today's Decisions for the Rest of Your Life. .* Nashville: Thomas Nelson Book Group.

Milonovich, G. M. (2011). Learning from Failure. *The FBI Law Enforcement Bulletin.*

Munroe, M. (1992). *In the Pursuit of Purpose.* Shippensburg: Desting Image

Niven, D. (2009). *100 Simple Secrets of Successful People.* San Francisco: Harper.

Schein, E. (2004). Organizational Culture and Leadership. San Francisco: John Wiley and Sons.

Soldera, S. (2002). The Individual Life Project: A New Way of Discovering the Unborn Child's World and Potentialities. *Birth Psychology*, May, 2002. 361-377. Retrieved from https://birthpsychology.com/journals/volume-16-issue-

4/individual-life-project-new-way-discovering-unborn-childs-world-and-potentialities.

Success Magazine (2009). Achieve Your Goals: Become The Person You Want to Be. October, 2009.

---

[i] Good Times, Produced by Norman Lear 1974-1979.

[ii] King James version of the Bible.

www.ingramcontent.com/pod-product-compliance
Lightning Source LLC
Chambersburg PA
CBHW060709030426
42337CB00017B/2817